Union Prayer-Book for Jewish Worship

Central Conference Of American Rabbis

סדר תפלות ישראל

The Union Prayer=Book

for

Jewish Worship

MORNING SERVICES

EDITED AND PUBLISHED

BY

THE CENTRAL CONFERENCE OF AMERICAN RABBIS

Provisional Edition

NEW YORK
1907

COPYRIGHT 1907

BY

THE CENTRAL CONFERENCE OF AMERICAN RABBIS

RESS OF
STETTINER BROS.,
NEW YORK

Preface

THIS book contains several services for Jewish worship. They are derived almost entirely from the traditional liturgy. The translations are selected from the Union Prayer Book, the Rev. S. Singer's issue of the Daily Prayer Book, and from the Order of Service of the Jewish Religious Union. The passages from the Bible are given according to the Revised Version. All the additional prayers, as well as the selection of Scripture verses, are adopted from the book of the Jewish Religious Union, to the editors of which the Committee is greatly indebted.

RESS OF
STETTINER BROS.,
NEW YORK

Contents

first Service

Minister:

MY God, the soul which Thou hast given me is pure. Thou didst create it and breathe it into me. Thou preservest it within me during my life on earth, and Thou wilt hereafter take it to life everlasting. As long as the soul is within me I will give thanks unto Thee, O Lord my God and God of my fathers, Sovereign of creation, Lord of all souls. Blessed art Thou, O Lord, who callest the dead to everlasting life.

Choir:—Amen.

Minister:

בָּרְכוּ אֶת יְיָ הַמְבֹרָךְ:

Praise ye the Lord, to whom all praise is due!

Choir and Congregation:

בָּרוּךְ יְיָ הַמְבֹרָךְ לְעוֹלָם וָעֶר:

Praised be the Lord from this time forth and forever.

Minister:

PRAISE be to Thee, O Lord, our God, Ruler of the world, who in Thy mercy causest light to shine over the earth and all its inhabitants, and daily renewest the works of creation. How manifold are Thy works, O Eternal; in wisdom hast Thou made them all; the earth is full of Thy possessions. The heavens declare Thy glory and the firmament showeth Thy handiwork. Thou formest light and darkness, ordainest good and evil, and bringest harmony into nature, and peace to the heart of man.

With love abounding hast Thou guided us, O our God, and with great compassion hast Thou borne with us. O our Father, our King, for our fathers' sake, who trusted in Thee, and whom Thou didst teach the statutes of life, be also gracious unto us and teach us. We beseech Thee, O merciful Father, to grant us discernment, that we may understand and fulfil all the teachings of Thy word. Make us gladly obedient to Thy commandments and fill our hearts with love and reverence for Thee. In Thee we put our trust; we rejoice and delight in Thy help; for with Thee alone is salvation. Thou hast called us as the teachers of Thy law; Thou hast chosen us for a holy mission unto mankind; therefore do we joyfully lift up our voices and proclaim Thy unity. Blessed be Thou, O God, who hast revealed Thy truth through Israel.

Choir:—Amen.

Minister, then Choir and Congregation:

שְׁמַע יִשְׂרָאֵל יְהֹוָה אֱלֹהֵינוּ יְהֹוָה אֶחָד:

Hear, O Israel, the Lord our God, the Lord is One.

בָּרוּךְ שֵׁם כְּבוֹד מַלְכוּתוֹ לְעוֹלָם וָעֶד:

Praised be His glorious name forever and ever.

Minister:

AND thou shalt love the Lord, thy God, with all thy heart, with all thy soul, and with all thy might. And these words, which I command thee this day, shall be in thy heart. Thou shalt teach them diligently unto thy children, and shalt speak of them when thou sittest in thy house, when thou walkest by the way, when thou liest down, and when thou risest up. Bind them as a sign upon thy hand, and let them be as frontlets between thine eyes. Write them upon the doorposts of thy house and upon thy gates.

To the end that ye may remember to do according to all my commandments and be holy unto your God.

Responsive Reading:

Minister.

TEACH me, O Lord, the way of Thy statutes; and I shall keep it unto the end.

Congregation.

Give me understanding, and I shall keep Thy law; yea, I shall observe it with my whole heart.

M. Make me to go in the path of Thy commandments; for therein do I delight.

C. Incline my heart unto Thy testimonies, and not to covetousness.

M. Turn away mine eyes from beholding vanity, and quicken me in Thy ways.

C. Confirm Thy word unto Thy servant, which belongeth unto the fear of Thee.

M. Turn away my reproach whereof I am afraid; for Thy judgments are good.

C. Behold, I have longed after Thy precepts; quicken me in Thy righteousness.

M. Let Thy mercies also come unto me, O Lord, even Thy salvation, according to Thy word.

C. So shall I have an answer for him that reproacheth me; for I trust in Thy word.

M. And take not the word of truth utterly out of my mouth; for I have hoped in Thy judgments.

C. So shall I observe Thy law continually forever and ever.

M. And I will walk at liberty; for I have sought Thy precepts.

C. I will also speak of Thy testimonies before kings, and will not be ashamed.

M. And I will delight myself in Thy commandments, which I have loved.

C. I will.lift up my hands also unto Thy commandments, which I have loved; and I will meditate in Thy statutes.

[Psalm cxix, 33-48.]

Choir:

Who is like unto Thee, O God, among the mighty?
Who is like unto Thee, glorious in holiness,
extolled in praises, working wonders?
God reigneth forever and ever.

Minister:

O Rock of Israel, be pleased to redeem those that are oppressed, and deliver those that are persecuted. Praise be unto Thee, our redeemer, the Holy One of Israel.

Choir:—Amen.

Minister:

PRAISE be unto Thee, O Eternal, our God, God of our fathers, Abraham, Isaac, and Jacob, the great, mighty, and most high God. Thou bestowest lovingkindness upon all Thy creatures; Thou rememberest the goodness of the fathers, and Thou sendest redemption to their descendants for the sake of Thy name. Thou art our helper, our redeemer and protector. Praise be to Thee, O God, shield of Abraham.

Thou art mighty, O Lord; Thine is the power to save. In Thy kindness Thou sustainest the living, upholdest the falling, healest the sick, and settest captives free. Thou wilt of a surety fulfil Thy promise of immortal life unto those who sleep in the dust. Who is like unto Thee, Almighty, author of life and death, source of salvation? Praise be to Thee, O God, who hast implanted within us immortal life.

Choir:—Amen.

SANCTIFICATION

(Congregation standing.)

Minister:

We hallow Thy name on earth, even as it is hallowed in heaven; and with the prophet say in humble adoration:

Holy, holy, holy is the Lord of hosts; the whole earth is full of His glory.

Choir and Congregation:

קָדוֹשׁ קָדוֹשׁ קָדוֹשׁ יְיָ צְבָאוֹת. מְלֹא כָל־הָאָרֶץ כְּבוֹדוֹ:

Minister:

In all places of Thy dominion Thy name is praised and glorified.

Choir and Congregation:

בָּרוּךְ כְּבוֹד יְיָ מִמְּקוֹמוֹ:

Minister:

God will reign forever, thy God, O Zion, from generation to generation. Hallelujah!

Choir and Congregation:

יִמְלֹךְ יְיָ לְעוֹלָם אֱלֹהַיִךְ צִיּוֹן לְדֹר וָדֹר הַלְלוּיָהּ:

(Congregation sitting.)

Silent Devotion:

O GOD, guard my tongue from evil and my lips from uttering deceit. Be my support when grief silences my voice, and my comfort when woe bends my spirit. Plant humility in my soul, and strengthen my heart with perfect faith in Thee. Help me to be strong when temptations and trials come, and to be meek when others wrong me, that I may readily forgive them. Guide me by the light of Thy counsel, and let me ever find rest in Thee, who art my strength and my redeemer. Amen.

Minister and Congregation together:

THE Lord is my shepherd; I shall not want. He maketh me to lie down in green pastures: He leadeth me beside the still waters. He restoreth my soul; He guideth me in the paths of righteousness for His name's sake. Yea, though I walk through the valley of the shadow of death I will fear no evil; for Thou art with me: Thy rod and Thy staff, they comfort me. Thou preparest a table before me in the presence of mine enemies: Thou has anointed my head with oil; my cup runneth over. Surely goodness and mercy shall follow me all the days of my life: and I will dwell in the house of the Lord forever. Amen.

Choir:

May the words of my mouth and the meditation of my heart be acceptable in Thy sight, O Lord, my strength and my redeemer.

Reading of Scripture

Choir:

The law of the Lord is perfect, restoring the soul: the testimony of the Lord is sure, making wise the simple. The precepts of the Lord are right, rejoicing the heart: the fear of the Lord is pure, enduring forever. Behold, a good doctrine has been given to you; forsake it not.

HYMN

SERMON

HYMN

ADORATION and KADDISH

(Page 56)

HYMN

BENEDICTION

Second Service

SOVEREIGN of all worlds! Not because of our righteous acts do we lay our supplications before Thee, but because of Thine abundant mercies. What are we? What is our life? What our righteousness? What our strength? What shall we say before Thee, O Lord our God and God of our fathers? Are not all the mighty men as naught before Thee, the men of renown as though they had not been, the wise as if without knowledge, and the men of understanding as if without discernment? For most of their works are void, and the days of their lives are vanity before Thee, and the pre-eminence of man over the beast is naught, for all is vanity; save only the pure soul, which will hereafter render its account before the throne of Thy glory. Nevertheless, we are Thy people, the children of Thy covenant, whose duty it is to offer praise and thanksgiving unto Thy name. Happy are we! How goodly is our portion, and how beautiful our heritage! Happy are we, who proclaim the unity of Thy name, as it is written: Hear, O Israel: the Lord our God, the Lord is One. Thou wast the same ere the world was created; Thou hast been the same since the world hath been created; Thou art the same in this world, and Thou wilt be the same in the world to come. Sanctify Thy Name upon them that sanctify it; yea, sanctify Thy Name throughout Thy world, and exalt us through Thy salvation.

Choir:—Amen.

15

Minister:

בָּרְכוּ אֶת יְיָ הַמְבֹרָךְ:

Praise ye the Lord, to whom all praise is due!

Choir and Congregation:

בָּרוּךְ יְיָ הַמְבֹרָךְ לְעוֹלָם וָעֶד:

Praised be the Lord from this time forth and forever.

Minister:

PRAISE be to Thee, O Lord, our God, Ruler of
the world, who in Thy mercy causest light to
shine over the earth and all its inhabitants, and daily
renewest the works of creation. How manifold are
Thy works, O Eternal; in wisdom hast Thou made
them all; the earth is full of Thy possessions. The
heavens declare Thy glory and the firmament showeth Thy handiwork. Thou formest light and darkness, ordainest good and evil, and bringest harmony
into nature, and peace to the heart of man.

With love abounding hast Thou guided us, O our
God, and with great compassion hast Thou borne
with us. O our Father, our King, for our fathers'
sake, who trusted in Thee, and whom Thou didst
teach the statutes of life, be also gracious unto us and
teach us. We beseech Thee, O merciful Father, to
grant us discernment, that we may understand and
fulfil all the teachings of Thy word. Make us gladly

obedient to Thy commandments and fill our hearts
with love and reverence for Thee. In Thee we put
our trust; we rejoice and delight in Thy help; for
with Thee alone is salvation. Thou hast called us as
the teachers of Thy law; Thou hast chosen us for a
holy mission unto mankind; therefore do we joyfully lift up our voices and proclaim Thy unity.
Blessed be Thou, O God, who hast revealed Thy
truth through Israel.

Choir:—Amen.

Minister, then Choir and Congregation:

שְׁמַע יִשְׂרָאֵל יְהֹוָה אֱלֹהֵינוּ יְהֹוָה אֶחָד:

Hear, O Israel, the Lord our God, the Lord is One.

בָּרוּךְ שֵׁם כְּבוֹד מַלְכוּתוֹ לְעוֹלָם וָעֶד:

Praised be His glorious name forever and ever.

Minister:

AND thou shalt love the Lord, thy God, with all thy
heart, with all thy soul, and with all thy might.
And these words, which I command thee this day,
shall be in thy heart. Thou shalt teach them diligently unto thy children, and shalt speak of them
when thou sittest in thy house, when thou walkest by
the way, when thou liest down, and when thou risest
up. Bind them as a sign upon thy hand, and let
them be as frontlets between thine eyes. Write them
upon the doorposts of thy house and upon thy gates.

To the end that ye may remember and do all my
commandments and be holy unto your God.

Responsive Reading:

Minister.

BLESS the Lord, O my soul. O Lord, my God, Thou art very great;

Congregation.

Thou art clothed with honor and majesty.

M. Who coverest Thyself with light as with a garment; who stretchest out the heavens like a curtain;

C. Who layeth the beams of His chambers in the waters;

M. Who maketh the clouds His chariot; who walketh upon the wings of the wind:

C. Who maketh winds His messengers; His ministers a flaming fire:

M. Who laid the foundations of the earth, that it should not be moved for ever.

C. Thou coveredst it with the deep as with a vesture; the waters stood above the mountains.

M. At Thy rebuke they fled; at the voice of Thy thunder they hasted away;

C. They rise among the mountains, they run down along the valleys, to the place which Thou hast appointed for them.

M. Thou hast set a bound that they may not pass over; that they turn not again to cover the earth.

C. He sendeth forth springs into the valleys; they run among the mountains:

M. They give drink to every beast of the field; the wild asses quench their thirst.

C. By them the fowl of the heaven have their habitation; they sing among the branches.

M. He watereth the mountains from His chambers: the earth is satisfied with the fruit of Thy works.

C. He causeth the grass to grow for the cattle, and herb for the service of man; that he may bring forth food out of the earth:

M. And wine that maketh glad the heart of man, and oil to make his face to shine, and bread that strengtheneth man's heart.

C. He appointed the moon for seasons: the sun knoweth his going down.

M. Thou makest darkness, and it is night; wherein all the beasts of the forest do creep forth.

C. The young lions roar after their prey, and seek their meat from God.

M. The sun ariseth, they get them away, and lay them down in their dens.

C. Man goeth forth unto his work and to his labor until the evening.

M. O Lord, how manifold are Thy works! In wisdom hast Thou made them all: the earth is full of Thy riches.

[Psalm civ, 1-24.]

Choir:

Who is like unto Thee, O God, among the mighty?
    Who is like unto Thee, glorious in holiness,
    extolled in praises, working wonders?
God reigneth forever and ever.

Minister:

O Rock of Israel, be pleased to redeem those that
are oppressed, and deliver those that are persecuted.
Praise be unto Thee, our redeemer, the Holy One of
Israel.

Choir:—Amen.

Minister:

PRAISE be to Thee, O Eternal, our God, God of
our fathers Abraham, Isaac, and Jacob, the
great, mighty, and most high God. Thou bestowest
lovingkindness upon all Thy creatures; Thou rememberest the goodness of the fathers, and Thou
sendest redemption to their descendants for the sake
of Thy name. Thou art our help, our redeemer and
protector. Praise be to Thee, O God, shield of
Abraham.

Thou art mighty, O Lord; Thine is the power to
save. In Thy kindness Thou sustainest the living,
upholdest the falling, healest the sick, and settest
captives free. Thou wilt, of a surety, fulfil Thy
promise of immortal life unto those who sleep in
the dust. Who is like unto Thee, Almighty, author

upholdest the falling, healest the sick, and settest captives free. Thou wilt, of a surety, fulfil Thy promise of immortal life unto those who sleep in the dust. Who is like unto Thee, Almighty, author of life and death, source of salvation. Praise be to Thee, O God, who hast implanted within us immortal life.

Choir:—Amen.

SANCTIFICATION

(Congregation standing.)

We hallow Thy name on earth, even as it is hallowed in heaven; and with the prophet say in humble adoration:

Holy, holy, holy is the Lord of hosts; the whole earth is full of His glory.

Choir and Congregation:

קָדוֹשׁ קָדוֹשׁ קָדוֹשׁ יְיָ צְבָאוֹת. מְלֹא כָל־הָאָרֶץ כְּבוֹדוֹ:

Minister:

In all places of Thy dominion Thy name is praised and glorified.

Choir and Congregation:

בָּרוּךְ כְּבוֹד יְיָ מִמְּקוֹמוֹ:

Minister:

God will reign forever, thy God, O Zion, from
generation to generation. Hallelujah!

Choir and Congregation:

יִמְלֹךְ יְיָ לְעוֹלָם אֱלֹהַיִךְ צִיּוֹן לְדֹר וָדֹר הַלְלוּיָה:

(Congregation sitting.)

Silent Devotion:

O GOD, guard my tongue from evil and my lips
from uttering deceit. Be my support when
grief silences my voice, and my comfort when woe
bends my spirit. Plant humility in my soul, and
strengthen my heart with perfect faith in Thee. Help
me to be strong when temptations and trials come,
and to be meek when others wrong me, that I may
readily forgive them. Guide me by the light of Thy
counsel, and let me ever find rest in Thee, who art
my strength and my redeemer. Amen.

Minister and Congregation together:

WE gratefully acknowledge, O Lord, our God,
that Thou art our creator and preserver, the
rock of our life and the shield of our help. We render thanks unto Thee, for our lives which are in Thy
hand, for our souls which are ever in Thy keeping,
for Thy wondrous providence, and for Thy con-
tinuous goodness, which Thou bestowest upon us
day by day. Truly, Thy mercies never fail, and Thy
lovingkindness never ceases. Therefore, in Thee
do we forever put our trust.

Choir:

May the words of my mouth and the meditation of my heart be acceptable in Thy sight, O Lord, my strength and my redeemer.

Reading of Scripture

Choir:

It is a tree of life to them that lay hold of it and the supporters thereof are happy. Its ways are ways of pleasantness and all its paths are peace.

HYMN

SERMON

HYMN

ADORATION and KADDISH

(Page 56)

HYMN

BENEDICTION

Fifth Service

Minister:

HOW lovely are Thy dwelling-places, O Lord of hosts; better is a day in Thy courts than a thousand elsewhere; happy are they who dwell in Thy house, they are continually praising Thee. Incline Thine ear, answer us, be gracious unto us, O God, and cause us to rejoice, for unto Thee we lift up our souls. Teach us Thy way that we may walk firmly in Thy truth. Show us Thy kindness, grant us Thy salvation. Be with us this day and at all times, O Thou, our God and our Father, our rock and our support. Amen.

Choir:—Amen.

Minister:

בָּרְכוּ אֶת יְיָ הַמְבֹרָךְ׃

Praise ye the Lord, to whom all praise is due!

Choir and Congregation:

בָּרוּךְ יְיָ הַמְבֹרָךְ לְעוֹלָם וָעֶד׃

Praised be the Lord from this time forth and forever.

Minister:

PRAISE be to Thee, O Lord, our God, Ruler of the world, who in Thy mercy causest light to shine over the earth and all its inhabitants, and daily renewest the works of creation. How manifold are Thy works, O Eternal; in wisdom hast Thou made them all; the earth is full of Thy possessions. The heavens declare Thy glory and the firmament showeth Thy handiwork. Thou formest light and darkness, ordainest good and evil, and bringest harmony into nature, and peace to the heart of man.

With love abounding hast Thou guided us, O our God, and with great compassion hast Thou borne with us. O our Father, our King, for our fathers' sake, who trusted in Thee, and whom Thou didst teach the statutes of life, be also gracious unto us and teach us. We beseech Thee, O merciful Father, to grant us discernment, that we may understand and fulfil all the teachings of Thy word. Make us gladly obedient to Thy commandments and fill our hearts with love and reverence for Thee. In Thee we put our trust; we rejoice and delight in Thy help; for with Thee alone is salvation. Thou hast called us as the teachers of Thy law; Thou hast chosen us for a holy mission unto mankind; therefore do we joyfully lift up our voices and proclaim Thy unity. Blessed be Thou, O God, who hast revealed Thy truth through Israel.

Choir:—Amen.

Minister, then Choir and Congregation:

שְׁמַע יִשְׂרָאֵל יְהוָֹה אֱלֹהֵינוּ יְהוָֹה אֶחָר׃

Hear, O Israel, the Lord our God, the Lord is One.

בָּרוּךְ שֵׁם כְּבוֹד מַלְכוּתוֹ לְעוֹלָם וָעֶד׃

Praised be His glorious name forever and ever.

Minister:

THOU shalt love the Lord, Thy God, with all thy
heart, with all thy soul, and with all thy might.
And these words, which I command thee this day,
shall be in thy heart. Thou shalt teach them diligently unto thy children, and shalt speak of them
when thou sittest in thy house, when thou walkest by
the way, when thou liest down, and when thou risest
up. Bind them as a sign upon thy hand, and let
them be as frontlets between thine eyes. Write them
upon the doorposts of thy house and upon thy gates.

To the end that ye may remember and do all my
commandments and be holy unto your God. I am
the Lord your God.

Responsive Reading:

Minister.

HAPPY are they who dwell in Thy house, they
shall continually praise Thee.

Congregation.

Happy are they who thus know Him; happy the
people whose God is the Eternal.

M. There is no speech nor language; their voice cannot be heard.

C. Their line is gone out through all the earth, and their words to the end of the world.

M. In them hath He set a tabernacle for the sun, which is as a bridegroom coming out of his chamber, and rejoiceth as a strong man to run his course.

C. His going forth is from the end of the heaven, and his circuit unto the ends of it: and there is nothing hid from the heat thereof.

M. The law of the Lord is perfect, restoring the soul: the testimony of the Lord is sure, making wise the simple.

C. The precepts of the Lord are right, rejoicing the heart; the commandment of the Lord is pure, enlightening the eyes.

M. The fear of the Lord is clean, enduring forever: the judgments of the Lord are true, and righteous altogether.

C. More to be desired are they than gold, yea, than much fine gold: sweeter also than honey and the honeycomb.

M. Moreover, by them is Thy servant warned: in keeping of them there is great reward.

C. Who can discern his errors? Clear Thou me from hidden faults.

M. Keep back Thy servant also from presumptuous sins; let them not have dominion over me:

C. The Lord is righteous in all His ways, and merciful in all His works.

M. The Lord is near to all who call upon Him, who call upon Him in truth.

C. He fulfilleth the desire of those that fear Him: He will hear their cry and save them.

M. My mouth shall praise the Lord; and let all flesh bless His holy name forever and ever.

C. Let us praise the Lord henceforth and forever. Hallelujah!   [Psalm cxlv.]

Choir:

Who is like unto Thee, O God, among the mighty?
Who is like unto Thee, glorious in holiness,
extolled in praises, working wonders?
God reigneth forever and ever.

Minister:

As Thou hast redeemed Israel and saved him from arms stronger than his, so mayest Thou redeem all who are oppressed and persecuted. Blessed art Thou, O God, redeemer of Israel.

Choir:—Amen.

Minister:

PRAISE be unto Thee, O Eternal, our God, God of our fathers Abraham, Isaac, and Jacob, the great, mighty, and most high God. Thou bestowest lovingkindness upon all Thy creatures; Thou rememberest the goodness of the fathers, and Thou sendest redemption to their descendants for the sake of Thy name. Thou art our helper, our redeemer and protector. Praise be to Thee, O God, shield of Abraham.

Thou art mighty, O Lord; Thine is the power to save. In Thy kindness Thou sustainest the living, upholdest the falling, healest the sick, and settest captives free. Thou wilt, of a surety, fulfil Thy promise of immortal life unto those who sleep in the dust. Who is like unto Thee, Almighty, author of life and death, source of salvation? Praise be to Thee, O God, who hast implanted within us immortal life.

SANCTIFICATION

(Congregation standing.)

Minister:

We hallow Thy name on earth, even as it is hallowed in heaven; and with the prophet say in humble adoration:

Holy, holy, holy is the Lord of hosts; the whole earth is full of His glory.

Choir and Congregation:

קָדוֹש קָדוֹש קָדוֹש יְיָ צְבָאוֹת. מְלֹא כָל הָאָרֶץ כְּבוֹדוֹ:

Minister:

In all places of Thy dominion Thy name is praised and glorified.

Choir and Congregation:

בָּרוּךְ כְּבוֹד יְיָ מִמְּקוֹמוֹ:

Minister:

God will reign forever, thy God, O Zion, from generation to generation. Hallelujah!

Choir and Congregation:

יִמְלֹךְ יְיָ לְעוֹלָם אֱלֹהַיִךְ צִיּוֹן לְדֹר וָדֹר הַלְלוּיָהּ:

(Congregation sitting.)

Silent Devotion:

O GOD, guard my tongue from evil and my lips from uttering deceit. Be my support when grief silences my voice, and my comfort when woe bends my spirit. Plant humility in my soul, and strengthen my heart with perfect faith in Thee. Help me to be strong when temptations and trials come, and to be meek when others wrong me, that I may readily forgive them. Guide me by the light of Thy counsel, and let me ever find rest in Thee, who art my strength and my redeemer. Amen.

Minister and Congregation together:

LET Thy lovingkindness, O Lord, be upon us, according as we have hoped for Thee. Save us, O God of our salvation, to give thanks unto Thy holy name, and to triumph in Thy praise. All nations whom Thou hast made shall come and worship before Thee, O Lord; and they shall glorify Thy name; for Thou art great and doest marvelous things; Thou art God alone. But we are Thy people and the sheep of Thy pasture; we will give thanks unto Thee forever: we will recount Thy praise to all generations. Amen.

Choir:

May the words of my mouth and the meditation
of my heart be acceptable in Thy sight, O Lord,
my strength and my redeemer.

Reading of Scripture

Choir:

It is a tree of life to them that lay hold of it and
the supporters thereof are happy.   Its ways are
ways of pleasantness and all its paths are peace.

HYMN

SERMON

HYMN

ADORATION and KADDISH

(Page 56)

HYMN

BENEDICTION

ADORATION
(Congregation standing.)
Minister:

LET us adore the ever-living God, and render praise unto Him who spread out the heavens and established the earth, whose glory is revealed in the heavens above and whose greatness is manifest throughout the world: He is our God; there is none else.

We bow our head and bend our knee and magnify the King of kings, the Holy One, the Ever-blest.

Choir and Congregation:

וַאֲנַחְנוּ כּוֹרְעִים וּמִשְׁתַּחֲוִים וּמוֹדִים לִפְנֵי מֶלֶךְ
מַלְכֵי הַמְּלָכִים הַקָּדוֹשׁ בָּרוּךְ הוּא:

(Congregation sitting.)
Minister:

MAY the time not be distant, O God, when Thy name shall be worshiped in all the earth, when unbelief shall disappear and error be no more. We fervently pray that the day may come upon which all men shall invoke Thy name, when corruption and evil shall give way to purity and goodness; when superstition shall no longer enslave the minds, nor idolatry blind the eyes; when all inhabitants of the earth shall perceive that to Thee alone every knee must bend and every tongue give homage. O may all, created in Thine image, recognize that they are brethren, so that they, one in spirit and one in fellowship, may be forever united before Thee.

Then shall Thy kingdom be established on earth, and the word of Thine ancient seer be fulfilled: The Eternal shall rule forever and aye.

Congregation:

On that day the Eternal shall be One, and His name
   shall be One.

Minister:

ALL you who mourn the loss of loved ones, and, at this hour, remember the goodness, the hope, and the sweet companionship that have passed away with them, give ear to the word of comfort spoken to you in the name of your God. Only the body has died and has been laid in the dust. The spirit lives and will live on forever. In this life, also, the loved ones continue in the remembrance of those to whom they were precious. Every act of goodness they performed, every true and beautiful word they spoke, is treasured up and becomes an incentive to actions by which the living honor the dead.

And when you ask in your grief: Whence shall come my help and my comfort? then, in the strength of faith, answer with the Psalmist: "My help cometh from God," who will not forsake me, nor leave me in my grief. Upon Him I cast my burden, and He will grant me strength according to the days He has apportioned to me. All souls are His, and no power can take them out of His hands. Come, then, and in the midst of sympathizing fellow-worshipers, rise, and hallow the name of God

EXTOLLED and hallowed be the name of God throughout the world which He has created, and which He governs according to His righteous will. Just is He in all His ways, and wise are all His decrees. May His kingdom come, and His will be done in all the earth.

Congregation:

Blessed be the Lord of life and righteous Judge for evermore.

Minister:

To the departed whom we now remember, may peace and bliss be granted in the world of eternal life. There may they find grace and mercy before the Lord of heaven and earth. May their souls rejoice in that ineffable good which God has laid up for those that fear Him, and may their memory be a blessing unto those that cherish it.

Congregation:
Amen.

Minister:

May the Father of peace send peace to all troubled souls, and comfort all the bereaved among us.

Congregation:
Amen.

(The mourners standing and speaking with the Minister.)

יִתְגַּדַּל וְיִתְקַדַּשׁ שְׁמֵהּ רַבָּא. בְּעָלְמָא דִּי־בְרָא
כִרְעוּתֵהּ. וְיַמְלִיךְ מַלְכוּתֵהּ. בְּחַיֵּיכוֹן וּבְיוֹמֵיכוֹן וּבְחַיֵּי
דְכָל בֵּית יִשְׂרָאֵל. בַּעֲגָלָא וּבִזְמַן קָרִיב. וְאִמְרוּ
אָמֵן:

Congregation:

יְהֵא שְׁמֵהּ רַבָּא מְבָרַךְ · לְעָלַם וּלְעָלְמֵי עָלְמַיָּא:

Minister:

יִתְבָּרַךְ וְיִשְׁתַּבַּח וְיִתְפָּאַר וְיִתְרוֹמַם וְיִתְנַשֵּׂא
וְיִתְהַדָּר וְיִתְעַלֶּה וְיִתְהַלָּל שְׁמֵהּ דְּקוּדְשָׁא. בְּרִיךְ
הוּא. לְעֵלָּא מִן כָּל בִּרְכָתָא וְשִׁירָתָא. תֻּשְׁבְּחָתָא
וְנֶחָמָתָא. דַּאֲמִירָן בְּעָלְמָא. וְאִמְרוּ אָמֵן:

עַל יִשְׂרָאֵל וְעַל צַדִּיקַיָּא. וְעַל־כָּל־מָן דְּאִתְפְּטַר
מִן עָלְמָא הָדֵין כִּרְעוּתֵהּ דֶּאֱלָהָא · יְהֵא לְהוֹן שְׁלָמָא
רַבָּא וְחוּלָקָא טָבָא לְחַיֵּי עָלְמָא דְּאָתֵי · וְחִסְדָּא
וְרַחֲמֵי מִן־קֳדָם מָרֵא שְׁמַיָּא וְאַרְעָא. וְאִמְרוּ אָמֵן:

יְהֵא שְׁלָמָא רַבָּא מִן־שְׁמַיָּא וְחַיִּים · עָלֵינוּ וְעַל־כָּל־
יִשְׂרָאֵל. וְאִמְרוּ אָמֵן:

עֹשֶׂה שָׁלוֹם בִּמְרוֹמָיו. הוּא יַעֲשֶׂה שָׁלוֹם עָלֵינוּ
וְעַל כָּל יִשְׂרָאֵל. וְאִמְרוּ אָמֵן:

Hymn

L ORD of the World, He reigned alone
 While yet the Universe was naught.
  When by His will all things were wrought,
Then first His sovran name was known.

And when the All shall cease to be,
 In dread lone splendor He shall reign.
 He was, He is, He shall remain
In glorious eternity.

For He is one, no second shares
 His nature or His loneliness;
 Unending and beginningless, .
All strength is His, all sway He bears.

He is the living God to save,
 My Rock while sorrow's toils endure,
 My banner and my stronghold sure,
The cup of life whene'er I crave.

I place my soul within His palm,
 Before I sleep as when I wake,
 And though my body I forsake,
Rest in the Lord in fearless calm.

Hymn

אֲדוֹן עוֹלָם אֲשֶׁר מָלַךְ ・ בְּטֶרֶם כָּל־יְצִיר נִבְרָא׃

לְעֵת נַעֲשָׂה בְחֶפְצוֹ כֹּל ・ אֲזַי מֶלֶךְ שְׁמוֹ נִקְרָא׃

וְאַחֲרֵי כִּכְלוֹת הַכֹּל ・ לְבַדּוֹ יִמְלוֹךְ נוֹרָא׃

וְהוּא הָיָה וְהוּא הֹוֶה ・ וְהוּא יִהְיֶה בְּתִפְאָרָה׃

וְהוּא אֶחָד וְאֵין שֵׁנִי ・ לְהַמְשִׁיל לוֹ לְהַחְבִּירָה׃

בְּלִי רֵאשִׁית בְּלִי תַכְלִית ・ וְלוֹ הָעֹז וְהַמִּשְׂרָה׃

וְהוּא אֵלִי וְחַי גֹּאֲלִי ・ וְצוּר חֶבְלִי בְּעֵת צָרָה׃

וְהוּא נִסִּי וּמָנוֹס לִי ・ מְנָת כּוֹסִי בְּיוֹם אֶקְרָא׃

בְּיָדוֹ אַפְקִיד רוּחִי ・ בְּעֵת אִישָׁן וְאָעִירָה׃

וְעִם רוּחִי גְּוִיָּתִי ・ יְיָ לִי וְלֹא אִירָא׃

hymn

WHO is like Thee, O universal Lord?
 Who dare Thy praise and glory share?
Who is in heaven, Most High, like Thee adored?
 Who can on earth with Thee compare?
 Thou art the One true God alone,
 And firmly founded is Thy throne.

Thy tender love embraces all mankind,
 As children all by Thee are blest;
Repentant sinners with Thee mercy find,
 Thy hand upholdeth the opprest;
 All worlds attest Thy power sublime,
 Thy glory shines in every clime.

And to Thy might and love is joined in Thee
 The highest wisdom's living spring;
Whate'er to us is deepest mystery,
 Is clear to Thee, our Lord and King.
 O God of wisdom, love, and might,
 We worship Thee, Eternal Light.

Hymn

אֵין כֵּאלֹהֵינוּ · אֵין כַּאדוֹנֵינוּ ·
אֵין כְּמַלְכֵּנוּ · אֵין כְּמוֹשִׁיעֵנוּ:

מִי כֵאלֹהֵינוּ · מִי כַאדוֹנֵינוּ ·
מִי כְמַלְכֵּנוּ · מִי כְמוֹשִׁיעֵנוּ:

נוֹדֶה לֵאלֹהֵינוּ · נוֹדֶה לַאדוֹנֵינוּ ·
נוֹדֶה לְמַלְכֵּנוּ · נוֹדֶה לְמוֹשִׁיעֵנוּ:

בָּרוּךְ אֱלֹהֵינוּ · בָּרוּךְ אֲדוֹנֵינוּ ·
בָּרוּךְ מַלְכֵּנוּ · בָּרוּךְ מוֹשִׁיעֵנוּ:

אַתָּה הוּא אֱלֹהֵינוּ · אַתָּה הוּא אֲדוֹנֵינוּ ·
אַתָּה הוּא מַלְכֵּנוּ · אַתָּה הוּא מוֹשִׁיעֵנוּ:

BENEDICTION

Minister:

OUR God, may Thy blessing rest upon us, according to the gracious promise of Thy word:

יְבָרֶכְךָ יְיָ וְיִשְׁמְרֶךָ:

May the Lord bless thee and keep thee!

Choir:—Amen.

יָאֵר יְיָ פָּנָיו אֵלֶיךָ וִיחֻנֶּךָ:

May the Lord let His countenance shine upon **thee** and be gracious unto thee!

Choir:—Amen.

יִשָּׂא יְיָ פָּנָיו אֵלֶיךָ וְיָשֵׂם לְךָ שָׁלוֹם:

May the Lord lift up His countenance upon thee and give thee peace!

Choir:—Amen.

Prayers and Selections

Additional Prayers

1

THE breath of every living being shall bless Thy name, O Lord our God, and the spirit of all flesh shall continually glorify and exalt Thee, O our King; from everlasting to everlasting Thou art God; and beside Thee we have no King who redeemeth and saveth, setteth free and delivereth, who supporteth and pitieth in all times of trouble and distress; yea, we have no King but Thee.

Thou art God of the first and of the last, the God of all creatures. the Lord of all generations, extolled with many praises, who guidest Thy world with lovingkindness and Thy creatures with tender mercies. Thou, O Lord, slumberest not, nor sleepest; Thou arousest the sleepers and awakenest the slumberers; Thou makest the dumb to speak, loosest the bound, supportest the falling, and raisest up those that are bowed down. To Thee alone we give thanks.

2

AND David blessed the Lord in the presence of all the congregation: and David said, Blessed art Thou, O Lord, the God of Israel our father, from everlasting to everlasting. Thine, O Lord, is the greatness, and the power, and the glory, and the victory, and the majesty: for all that is in the heaven and in the earth is Thine; Thine, O Lord, is the kingdom, and the supremacy as head over all. Riches and honor come of Thee, and Thou rulest over all; and in Thine hand are might and power; and in Thine hand it is to make great, and to give strength unto all. Now, therefore, our God, we give thanks unto Thee, and praise Thy glorious name.

Thou art the Lord, even Thou alone; Thou hast made the heavens, the heaven of heavens, and all their host, the earth and all things that are thereon, the seas and all that is in them, and Thou givest life to them all; and the host of heaven worship Thee.

[I Chron. xxix, 10–13.]

3

BLESSED be the Lord by day; blessed be the Lord by night; blessed be the Lord when we lie down; blessed be the Lord when we rise up. For in Thy hand are the souls of the living and the dead; as it is said, In His hand is the soul of every living thing, and the spirit of all human flesh. Into Thy hand I commend my spirit; Thou hast redeemed me, O Lord God of truth. Our God, who art in heaven, assert the unity of Thy name, and establish Thy kingdom, and reign over us forever and ever.

4

FOR the first and for the last ages Thy Word is good and endureth forever and ever; it is true and trustworthy, a statute which shall not pass away. True it is that Thou art indeed the Lord our God and the God of our fathers, our King, our fathers' King, our Redeemer, the Redeemer of our fathers, our Maker, the Rock of our salvation; our Deliverer and Rescuer throughout the ages, such is Thy name; there is no God beside Thee.

Thou hast been the help of our fathers from of old, a Shield and Savior to their children after them in every generation. Thy judgments and Thy righteousness reach to the furthest ends of the earth. Happy is the man who hearkeneth unto Thy commandments, and layeth up Thy Law and Thy word in his heart. True it is that Thou art indeed the Lord of Thy people and a mighty King to defend their cause. True it is that Thou art indeed the first and Thou art the last, and beside Thee we have no King, Redeemer and Savior. From Egypt Thou didst redeem us, O Lord our God, from the house of bondmen Thou didst deliver us, and from every enemy to our peace Thou hast rescued us. Wherefore we offer praises and thanks-givings to our God, who is high and exalted, great and revered; who bringeth low the haughty, and raiseth up the lowly, leadeth forth the prisoners, redeemeth the meek, helpeth the poor, and answereth His people when they cry unto Him. Amen.

5

ALMIGHTY and all-merciful God, whose hand is ever outstretched to uphold and guide all who seek Thee in sincerity of heart, do Thou in this sacred hour help us to find our way to Thee. We commend to Thy providential care this assembly of Thy people, gathered here in the hope that a common worship may prove helpful to them in their desire to serve and honor Thee. Pardon our shortcomings and offences; we know they are many and grievous. But let them not keep us from that communion with Thee without which our life is one long discord. Accept our prayers, however feeble and faltering, and grant that they may aid in fostering a spirit of true devotion among us, in uniting some at least of the scattered children of Israel, in binding them in a true spiritual harmony to one another and to Thee. Amen.

6

LORD, we pray to Thee on behalf of the whole house of Israel scattered over the face of the globe, destined, in every condition of their existence, to endure many a sharp trial of their faith. We beseech Thee so to aid and inspire them that neither in prosperity nor in adversity they be untrue to their mission; and even as Thou hast never deserted Thy people for Thy great name's sake, so may they never be unfaithful to Thee, but may show forth Thy glory and Thy goodness among the nations, testifying by their lives to the great and holy truths which Thou hast entrusted to them, and proving that happy is the people whose God is the Lord. Amen.

7

THOU whose infinite power and wisdom are reflected in the infinite varieties of Thy creation, we see Thy handiwork also in the differences that prevail in the minds of men. We pray to Thee for all men, Thy children, our brethren. Take them all under the sheltering wings of Thy love. And may we, recognising that divergencies of thought and belief are of Thine implanting, strive the more zealously to be one in charity and forbearance, one in the desire to know and do Thy will. Amen.

8

ALMIGHTY GOD, Thou who hearest prayer, Thou to whom we, Thy children, come with the burden of our sorrows and the tribute of our thanksgiving, fully trusting that Thou wilt sustain us with Thy comfort, and accept our glad homage—listen to us, we beseech Thee, in this solemn hour. Bless our worship today. May the gleams of Thy light, the visions of Thy truth, which have come to bless our souls this day, abide with us when we have gone hence and are mingling with the world, so that, whatever our trials, we may still hold fast to our faith in Thee, and whatever our temptations, we may still feel the sanctifying influence of Thy presence.

O God, we beseech Thee to be with us in the coming days of toil. Give us strength to bear our load of care; give us clearness of vision, so that we may see the wisdom and the love that has laid it upon us. Teach us to hallow our joys with thankfulness and our labor with righteousness. Help us to be true to our better selves, to discern our real work in life, and to do it with all our might. Be by our side when we are struggling with our own hearts, when we seek to rise above our failings and our weaknesses. Help us to realise life's meaning, to understand its solemnity, so that each day we live may be yet another step, leading us nearer and nearer to Thee. Amen.

9

MAY it be Thy will, O Lord our God, and the God of our fathers, to purify our thoughts and to enable us to give fit expression to them. Restrain us from pride; free us from error. Forgive all our iniquities. Be with our heart when we meditate how to address Thee, and with our lips when we utter our prayers, so that we say no word which is not in accordance with Thy will. Be with our hand when we labor. Let not the evil inclination be a source of stumbling to us, but be Thou with us lest we go astray.

Do Thou help us for the glory of Thy name, and be gracious unto us. Make Thy face to shine upon us, and impart of Thy glory unto us.

In this shall we know that Thou hast shown loving-kindness unto us, and delightest in us, and that Thou hast ordained that we shall stand in Thy presence in eternity.

10

Minister. ALMIGHTY GOD, source of all goodness and happiness, to whom no service is more precious than that of a cheerful and grateful spirit, we offer Thee our heartfelt thanks for the numberless tokens of Thy love with which our life is crowded. For the gift of life itself with all its possibilities, for the soul with all its faculties and endowments, and especially its power to recognise and confess Thee as the Author of all things :—

Cong.—We bless and praise Thee, Our heavenly Father.

Minister.—For the revelation of Thy will, and for the wise and loving ordinances which Thou hast designed for our guidance, enlightenment, and comfort; for the prophets and teachers of Israel who shine as the brightness of the firmament, and, having led many to righteousness, are like the stars forever; for the great and good of all ages, lands, and peoples who were faithful to the best they

knew, whose life's thought and work have become inter-
fused with the world's life, and upon whose inheritance we
have entered:—

Cong.—We bless and praise Thee, Our heavenly Father.

Minister.—For all the pleasant things of the earth: for
the beauty in which Thou hast robed Thy creation; for the
gift of health; for the joys of home and family; for the
blessing of little children; for the sweet communion of
friendship; for the intellectual delights Thou hast made
accessible to us; and for all the promptings of goodness
and purity, of tenderness and forbearance, of unselfishness
and brotherly love, which prepare the way on earth for the
kingdom of God:—

Cong.—We bless and praise Thee, Our heavenly Father.

Minister.—Help us, O Lord our God, to make a right use
of these and all Thy gifts. Sanctify unto us every earnest
effort we make, even as we do at this hour, to remember
some part of what we owe Thee, to the end that we may
live more worthily in Thy sight, and in seeking the welfare
and the happiness of Thy children, may serve Thee, as
Thou desirest, our heavenly Father. Amen.

II

Minister.—ALMIGHTY GOD: not in reliance upon
any merits of our own do we venture
to lay our petitions before Thee, but
sustained by Thy gracious promises and trusting to Thine
unfathomable mercies. May we never lose the sense of
Thy loving presence. In every trial and temptation of our
life may we look to Thee and not be ashamed.

When heavy burdens oppress us, or when we are dis-
heartened in our tasks, and our spirit faints within us, and
the gloom of failure settles upon us:—

Cong.—Lift up the light of Thy countenance upon us,
O Lord, and strengthen us.

Minister.—When the shadow of sickness, sorrow, or suffering falls upon us or our dear ones, and hides Thee from our vision:—

Cong.—Lift up the light of Thy countenance upon us, O Lord, and give us hope.

Minister.—When doubts assail us concerning Thy providence, Thy justice, and Thy goodness; when we question the value of this earthly life, and the reality of the heavenly, and our soul wanders in darkness, groping vainly for the place of her rest:—

Cong.—Lift up the light of Thy countenance upon us, O Lord, and solve our doubts.

Minister.—When, through self-indulgence, or from a blind following of the multitude, or by deliberate suppression of the voice of conscience, our sense of duty grows dim, and we call good evil and evil good, and the darkness light and the light darkness:—

Cong.—Lift up the light of Thy countenance upon us, O Lord, and give us discernment.

Minister.—When, immersed in sordid cares, or in the eager pursuit of wordly aims and pleasures, the very thought of Thee fades out of our consciousness:—

Cong.—Lift up the light of Thy countenance upon us, O Lord, and lead back our souls to Thy presence.

Minister.—And when there is a stirring within us of a better spirit, and a healthy discontent seizes upon us and bids us rise above our sinful selves, and we strive as best we can to raise our soul out of the dark abyss to our Father who is in Heaven, then come Thou to meet us, to cheer and hearten us:

Cong.—Lift up the light of Thy countenance upon us, O Lord, and bring back life to our soul.

Minister.—O God, in the abundance of Thy lovingkindness, answer us with Thy true salvation. Amen.

12

"LORD, my heart is not haughty, nor mine eyes lofty; neither do I exercise myself in great matters, on in things too wonderful for me."

O God, we feel Thine immeasurable greatness, and we know that if Thine ordinances are sometimes too hard for us to understand, it is because we lack the needful insight. Stern seems Thy face to us at times, but surely it is because we see Thee through the mists, with eyes that are weak and dim. Who are we that we should judge Thee? Shall the clay say to him that fashioneth it, What makest thou? Rather will we turn our gaze from the decrees that veil Thy goodness to those that reveal it; and, where we cannot know, we will be content to trust. Yes, we will still and quiet our soul as a little child with his mother. We will submit ourselves wholly to Thee in the full assurance that with Thee we are safe, and that shielded by Thine everlasting arms no real hurt can come to us. Though we walk through the valley of the shadow, we will fear no evil, for Thou art with us, and often what seems to be evil Thy wondrous love transforms into good.

O God, Thy faithful acts towards us are many, and that our soul knoweth right well. They are more than we can count, more than we deserve. To Thee we owe our life and the joys that weave themselves into it; to Thee we owe our loved ones, with all the delight their companionship yields us. Thy goodness has clothed the world outside us in glorious raiment, and given us the power to feel its splendor. To Thee we owe the pleasures of the mind, the solace of books, the ennobling influence of art, the joys of communion with the great souls of Israel and of mankind at large. And to Thee we owe, above all, the instinctive sense of Thy presence, the stir of the spirit which bids us seek after Thee, the lofty aspirations which lift us above the concerns of the sordid life into an ampler and a purer atmosphere.

For all these boons accept our fervent thanks, we beseech Thee, O God. We praise Thee for them for their own sake, for the sake of all the blessing we draw from them. But we praise Thee for them too because of the light they give us amid our darkness, because of the revelation of Thy goodness with which they uphold our fainting spirit. For merciful as Thou art to us in our joys, so merciful art Thou to us in our sorrows. Thy love for us is as strong when Thou dost thwart our will as when Thou workest to fulfil our wishes. And when we seem most forsaken of Thee, then indeed art Thou very near us.

O Father in Heaven, help us to engrave these dutiful thoughts ever deeply upon our hearts. Help us to hope in Thee from this time forth and for evermore. Amen.

13

OUR FATHER! Come Thou into our midst and give us hope. In Thy service we try to labor, in Thy love we put our trust. O Lord, have mercy! Awaken in our hearts gratitude for the burdens which Thou hast laid upon us. Give us strength to work out our lives fearlessly and faithfully.

Come to us, and show us the dignity and destiny of our work, which is dedicated unto Thee.

Our Father, we thank Thee for the manifold revelations of Thy lovingkindness, and especially for having placed in our hearts faith in a noble future for the sons of men whom Thou didst create in Thine image! May we strive now and henceforth to work honestly and well; to love and help our fellow-men, and in all the duties of our daily life to look to Thee for inspiration and discernment.

Let us never sink into indifference or idleness, for Thou hast created us in order that we may seek by diligent effort to approach nearer Thy Throne. Have pity on our weakness, and let us not fall by the way. In all we do, and in all we try to do, may we ever set Thee before us! We, who have our hope in Thee, our God, can never despair: for us failure has no terror. We feel Thy presence, and are at peace. Amen.

14

O LORD, Thou knowest all my desire, before ever my lips utter it. I ask for Thy favor but for a moment, then let me pass away. Would that my prayer were granted, so that I might entrust the remnant of my spirit into Thy hand; I would sleep, and sweet would be my repose. If I am far from Thee, my life is death, but if I cleave unto Thee, even in death I live. But I know not wherewith to come before Thee, or what shall be my service and my due. Teach me Thy ways, O Lord, and release me from the bondage of folly. Yea, teach me whilst yet I have the power to deny myself, and despise not my affliction; before the day cometh, when I shall be a burden to myself, and when of my body each part will lie heavy upon the other. Then shall I be humbled against my will, and corruption will consume my bones so that they will be too weary to bear me up. Then shall I go to the place whither my fathers went, and my lodging will be as theirs. I am as a stranger who tarrieth on the face of the earth, but within her bosom is my abiding inheritance. Hitherto my youthful passions have worked their will, but when shall I provide for my true self? The love of the world, which is set in my heart, hath prevented me from considering my end. How shall I serve my Maker, whilst yet I am the captive of my passions and the slave of my desires? How shall I seek to be of high degree when tomorrow "the worm may be my sister"? How can my heart be merry on a day of joy when I know not how it will be with me on the morrow? The days and nights are pledged to consume my flesh, until I fade away; part of me they will fling to the winds, and part they will bring back to the dust. What then shall I say, seeing that my passions pursue me as an enemy from youth to age? What hath time to give me except Thy favor, and if Thou art not my portion what is my portion? I am stripped bare of all good

deeds, and Thy righteousness alone is my covering. But
why need I prolong my prayer? Already, O Lord, Thou
knowest all my desire. Amen.

15

O LORD! Do Thou look with compassion on those
of us who are suffering from sickness, ignorance,
misery, or sin! Quicken us to a new life! Open
our eyes to find the best in life, the best in one another, so
that we may rejoice in Thy presence, and learn to serve
Thee by our happiness. Rouse those who tyrannise over
their fellow-men to a consciousness of their guilt! Soften
their hearts and bring pity into their souls. Show them
that the gift of power comes from Thee, and must be used
in Thy service. Let them not exalt themselves in vain
self-glory! Give us courage to resist cruelty and injustice,
for they are hateful in Thy sight. Have mercy, O Lord,
upon those who are being persecuted for their faith in
Thee, who suffer from the hands of men blinded with
ignorance and arrogance. O listen to the cry of the un-
happy!

Strengthen the bonds which unite men in Thy service,
and speed the time when the law of duty and the law of
love may enthral the whole world! Amen.

16

ALMIGHTY FATHER! We humbly ask Thee for
Thy help, for our need is great. O do Thou grant
peace to our souls. Our days fly past in quick suc-
cession, and are marked by happy expectations or by
grievous disappointments. With Thee, O Lord, is peace.
Our spirits are overwhelmed by the sense of our own shortcomings; we cannot look into the past without regret, or
into the future without misgiving.

O Lord, in the thought of Thy constant love and pity
may we learn to find our rest. We are weary with trying
to understand the mysteries of sin and of evil against

which we so often struggle in vain. Teach us to be still
and to wait patiently for Thee, who art perfect in knowledge and goodness. Amen.

17

O GOD, may our worship this day make us feel more
strongly than ever that Thou art our Father, and let
the thought of Thee help us to lead truer, gentler,
nobler lives. Thou art near to us, to each one of us, and
Thou wilt help us if we only try to do what we believe to
be right. In the trials and difficulties of the week before
us, be Thou our Guide and our Shield. Strengthen our
efforts, O Lord, to approach a little nearer unto Thee.

If our faith should fail us, if we should fall into temptation, do Thou make Thy presence felt, and give us courage
to arise and do Thy bidding. At this sacred hour every
thought of ours, every wish, is directed unto Thee; and
Thou, All-knowing and All-seeing God, understandest our
weakness, and hast pity on us. Thou wilt give us strength
to serve Thee. O Lord, help us to testify in our lives to
the love we bear Thee. Amen.

The Ten Commandments

1. I AM the Lord thy God, who brought thee out of the land of Egypt, out of the house of bondage.

2. Thou shalt have no other gods before me. Thou shalt not make unto thee a graven image, nor the form of anything that is in heaven above, or that is in the earth beneath, or that is in the water under the earth: thou shalt not bow down thyself unto them, nor serve them: for I the Lord thy God am a jealous God, visiting the iniquity of the fathers upon the children, upon the third and upon the fourth generation, of them that hate me; and showing mercy unto the thousandth generation, of them that love me and keep my commandments.

3. Thou shalt not take the name of the Lord thy God in vain; for the Lord will not hold him guiltless that taketh His name in vain.

4. Remember the sabbath day, to keep it holy. Six days shalt thou labor, and do all thy work: but the seventh day is a sabbath unto the Lord thy God: in it thou shalt not do any work: thou, nor thy son, nor thy daughter, thy manservant, nor thy maidservant, nor thy cattle, nor thy stranger that is within thy gates: for in six days the Lord made heaven and earth, the sea, and all that is therein, and rested the seventh day: wherefore the Lord blessed the sabbath day, and hallowed it.

5. Honor thy father and thy mother: that thy days may be long upon the land which the Lord thy God giveth thee.

6. Thou shalt not murder.

7. Thou shalt not commit adultery.

8. Thou shalt not steal.

9. Thou shalt not bear false witness against thy neighbor.

10. Thou shalt not covet thy neighbor's house, thou shalt not covet thy neighbor's wife, nor his manservant, nor his maidservant, nor his ox, nor his ass, nor any thing that is thy neighbor's.

Scripture Verses

A.

1. Know therefore this day, and lay it to thine heart, that the Lord He is God in heaven above and upon the earth beneath: there is none else. (Deuteronomy iv. 39.)

2. And now, Israel, what doth the Lord thy God require of thee, but to fear the Lord thy God, to walk in all His ways, and to love Him, and to serve the Lord thy God with all thy heart and with all thy soul, to keep the commandments of the Lord and His statutes, which I command thee this day for thy good? (Deuteronomy x. 12, 13.)

3. For this commandment which I command thee this day, it is not too hard for thee, neither is it far off. It is not in heaven, that thou shouldest say, Who shall go up for us to heaven, and bring it unto us, and make us to hear it, that we may do it? Neither is it beyond the sea, that thou shouldest say, Who shall go over the sea for us, and bring it unto us, and make us to hear it, that we may do it? But the word is very nigh unto thee, in thy mouth, and in thy heart, that thou mayest do it. (Deuteronomy xxx. 11-14.)

4. Thou shalt not go up and down as a tale-bearer among thy people. (Leviticus xix. 16.)

5. Thou shalt not hate thy brother in thy heart. (Leviticus xix. 17.)

6. Ye shall do no unrighteousness in judgment, in meteyard, in weight or in measure. (Leviticus xix. 35.)

7. Ye shall not steal, neither deal falsely, neither lie one to another. (Leviticus xix. 11.)

8. Love ye the stranger: for ye were strangers in the land of Egypt. Thou shalt not oppress a stranger, for ye know the heart of a stranger, seeing ye were strangers in the land of Egypt. If a stranger sojourn with thee in your land, ye shall not oppress him. The stranger that dwelleth with you shall be unto you as one born among you, and thou shalt love him as thyself. (Deuteronomy x. 19. Exodus xxiii. 9. Leviticus xix. 33, 34.)

9. Thou shalt not harden thine heart, nor shut thine hand from thy poor brother: but shalt surely open thine hand unto him, to lend him sufficient for his need in that which he wanteth. Thou shalt open wide thine hand unto thy brother that is needy and to thy poor in the land. And the stranger, and the fatherless, and the widow which are within thy gates shall come and shall eat and be satisfied; that the Lord thy God may bless thee in all the work of thy hand which thou doest. (Deuteronomy xv. 7, 8, 11; xiv. 29.)

10. Ye shall be holy: for I the Lord your God am holy. (Leviticus xix. 2.)

11. If ye will obey my voice indeed, and keep my covenant, then ye shall be a peculiar treasure unto me out of all the peoples: for all the earth is mine: and ye shall be unto me a kingdom of priests, and a holy nation. (Exodus xix. 5, 6.)

12. Thou shalt not avenge, nor bear any grudge against the children of thy people, but thou shalt love thy neighbor as thyself: I am the Lord. (Leviticus xix, 18.)

Blessed art Thou, O Lord, our God, King of the Universe, who hast given us Thy law of Truth, and planted in our midst eternal life.

B.

1. But now thus saith the Lord that created thee, O Jacob, and He that formed thee, O Israel: Fear not, for I have redeemed thee; I have called thee by thy name, thou art mine. (Isaiah xliii. 1.)

2. Ye are my witnesses, saith the Lord, and my servant whom I have chosen. (Isaiah xliii. 10.)

3. Behold my servant, whom I uphold: my chosen, in whom my soul delighteth: I have put my spirit upon him: he shall bring forth judgment to the nations. He shall not clamor nor cry, nor cause his voice to be heard in the street. A bruised reed shall he not break, and a dimly burning wick shall he not quench: he shall bring forth judgment faithfully. He shall not burn dimly, nor shall he be crushed, till he have set judgment in the earth; and the isles shall wait for his teaching. (Isaiah xlii. 1-4.)

4. And now saith the Lord that formed me to be His servant: It is too light a thing that thou shouldest be my servant to raise up the tribes of Jacob, and to restore the preserved of Israel: I will also give thee for a light to the nations, that my salvation may be unto the end of the earth. (Isaiah xlix. 5, 6.)

5. As for me, this is my covenant with them, saith the Lord: My spirit that is upon thee, and my words which I have put in thy mouth, shall not depart out of thy mouth, nor out of the mouth of thy seed, nor out of the mouth of thy seed's seed, saith the Lord, from henceforth and for ever. (Isaiah lix. 21.)

6. And it shall come to pass in the latter days, that the mountain of the Lord's house shall be established in the top of the mountains, and shall be exalted above the hills; and all nations shall flow into it. And many peoples shall go and say, Come ye, and let us go up to the mountain of the Lord, to the house of the God of Jacob; and He will teach us of His ways, and we will walk in His paths: for out of Zion shall go forth the law, and the word of the Lord from Jerusalem. (Isaiah ii. 2, 3.)

7. And the earth shall be full of the knowledge of the Lord, as the waters cover the sea. (Isaiah xi. 9.)

8. Then will I restore to the peoples a pure language, that they may all call upon the name of the Lord, to serve Him with one accord. (Zephaniah iii. 9.)

9. And they shall beat their swords into ploughshares, and their spears into pruning hooks: nation shall not lift up sword against nation, neither shall they learn war any more. (Isaiah ii. 4.)

10. And the Lord shall be king over all the earth: in that day the Lord shall be one, and His name one. (Zechariah xiv. 9.)

BLESSED art Thou, O Lord our King, King of the universe, Rock of all worlds, righteous through all generations, O faithful God, who sayest and doest, who speakest and fulfillest, all whose words are truth and righteousness. Faithful art Thou, O Lord our God, and faithful are Thy words, and not one of Thy words shall return void, for Thou art a faithful and merciful God and King. Blessed art Thou, O Lord God, who art faithful in all Thy words.

C.

1. Let justice roll down as waters, and righteousness as a perpetual stream. (Amos v. 24.)

2. I desire love, and not sacrifice; the knowledge of God, rather than burnt offerings. (Hosea vi. 6.)

3. These are the things that ye shall do: speak ye every man the truth with his neighbor: execute the judgment of truth and peace in your gates: and let none of you imagine evil in your hearts against his neighbor; and love no false oath: for all these are things that I hate, saith the Lord. (Zechariah viii. 16, 17.)

4. Repent, and turn yourselves from all your transgressions: so shall they not be a stumbling block of guilt unto you. Cast away from you all your transgressions,

wherein ye have transgressed; and make you a new heart and a new spirit: for why will ye die, O house of Israel? For I have no pleasure in the death of him that dieth, saith the Lord God; wherefore turn yourselves and live. (Ezekiel xviii, 30-32.)

5. A new heart will I give you, and a new spirit will I put within you: and I will take away the stony heart out of your flesh, and will give you a heart of flesh, and I will put my spirit within you. (Ezekiel xxxvi. 26, 27.)

6. Seek good, and not evil, that ye may live. Hate the evil, and love the good, and establish justice in the gate. (Amos v. 14, 15.)

7. Keep thy tongue from evil, and thy lips from speaking guile. Depart from evil, and do good; seek peace, and pursue it. (Psalm xxxiv. 13, 14.)

8. He hath showed thee, O man, what is good; and what doth the Lord require of thee, but to do justly, and to love mercy, and to walk humbly with thy God? (Micah vi. 8.)

9. Thou desirest not sacrifice, else would I give it: Thou delightest not in burnt offerings. The sacrifices of God are a broken spirit: a broken and a contrite heart, O God, Thou wilt not despise. (Psalm li. 17.)

10. Be glad in the Lord, and rejoice, ye righteous: and shout for joy, all ye that are upright in heart. (Psalm xxxii. 11.)

D.

1. Create in me a clean heart, O God; renew a steadfast spirit within me. Cast me not away from Thy presence; take not Thy holy spirit from me. (Psalm li. 10, 11.)

2. Teach me to do Thy will, for Thou art my God. Let Thy good spirit lead me in the right path. (Psalm cxliii. 10.)

3. Whither shall I go from Thy spirit? or whither shall I flee from Thy presence? If I ascend up into heaven, Thou are there: if I make my bed in the nether-world, behold, Thou art there. If I should take the wings of the morning, and alight in the uttermost parts of the sea, even there would Thy hand lead me, and Thy right hand would hold me. (Psalm cxxxix. 7-10.)

4. Whom have I in heaven but Thee? and there is nought upon earth that I desire beside Thee. My flesh and my heart may fail; but God is the rock of my heart and my portion forever. (Psalm lxxiii. 25, 26.)

5. Thou hast been my help, and in the shadow of Thy wings do I rejoice. My soul clingeth fast unto Thee: Thy right hand upholdeth me. (Psalm lxiii. 7, 8.)

6. If I think, 'My foot slippeth,' Thy lovingkindness, O Lord, holdeth me up. In the multitude of my cares within me, Thy comforts delight my soul. (Psalm xciv. 19.)

7. As the hart panteth after the water brooks, so panteth my soul after Thee, O God. (Psalm xlii. 1.)

8. How precious is Thy lovingkindness, O God! The children of men take refuge under the shadow of Thy wings. They feast upon the fatness of Thy house; and Thou makest them drink of the river of Thy pleasures. For with Thee is the fountain of life; through Thy light we see light. (Psalm xxxvi. 7-9.)

9. The Lord is my light and my salvation; whom shall I fear? The Lord is the fortress of my life: of whom shall I be afraid? (Psalm xxvii. 1.)

10. I have set the Lord always before me; with Him at my right hand I cannot be moved. (Psalm xvi. 8.)

CPSIA information can be obtained at www.ICGtesting.com
Printed in the USA
BVOW09s1932180515

400865BV00002B/3/P